# Acknowledgements

Much of the material for this book is the result of searches in local archives of the Hornsey Historical Society and Bruce Castle Museum, as well as the London Metropolitan Archives and the National Archives. All the people from these archives deserve many thanks for their patience and help. As well as these archives, a number of private collectors have generously given me permission to reproduce images, and thanks to them as acknowledged in the captions to the pictures.

# Contents

# 1

# Introduction

❦

Harringay, in the Borough of Haringey, as we know it today developed between 1880 and 1900 for a variety of reasons. A decline in local agricultural activity, in the face of produce brought quickly and cheaply to London on the railways, meant that former agricultural land was relatively cheap compared with land in the suburbs closer in to London. The conditions in London were also becoming overcrowded and the clearances for railway and other developments within the city exacerbated the problems. For many landowners on the fringes of London, it became financially attractive to sell land for building to accommodate the many people needing places to live. Speculative developers saw the possibility of exploiting the demand for new housing outside the metropolitan districts and were keen to promote new developments around the new transport connections to the city.

Harringay before 1880 was largely open fields and parkland with a road called Green Lanes across it. (Fig 1) This road is the path of an ancient route from Newington Green through Beans Green, past West Green, on to Wood Green, and then out to Palmers Green. Not surprisingly, the road connecting all these greens should have come to be called Green Lanes in the eighteenth century . Before 1880 there were virtually no buildings along Green Lanes, north of the Seven Sisters Road, which was bordered by a narrow strip of common, or waste land, known as Beans Green. The road and the wasteland lay between the fields of St John's

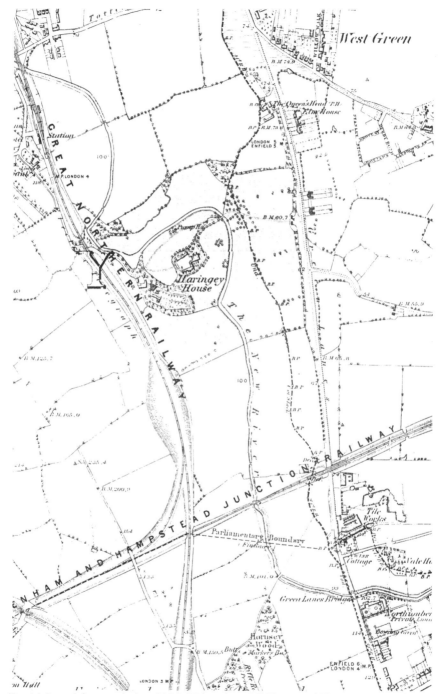

Fig 1 Map of the area before 1880 (Taken from HHS map of Hornsey in 1870)

Farm, in Tottenham, on the east, and the parkland and fields of the Harringay [Haringey] House, in Hornsey, on the west.

The Manor House public house was built in 1832 at the junction of Green Lanes and the newly constructed Seven Sisters Road. It took the name because it became the meeting place for the Vestry of Stoke Newington; it was never a manor house. Close by was Northumberland House, built in 1822 and converted into a Lunatic Asylum under the Mad House Act of 1929. Vivienne Eliot, the first wife of T.S. Eliot, was committed to Northumberland House in July 1938, where she died in 1947; the building was demolished in 1955. The New River, built by Hugh Myddelton and opened in 1613, was the longest aqueduct supplying fresh water to London. The aqueduct followed the contours of the landscape and meandered through the parkland of Harringay House to cross Green Lanes just below Northumberland House by the Bowling Green that stood on its banks.

Finsbury Park, opened in 1869, was designed by Alexander McKenzie, who also laid out Alexandra Park. The park largely covered the old Hornsey Wood, a favourite London recreation ground since the eighteenth century, and swept away the Hornsey Wood Tavern that stood at the crest of the hill. Endymion Road was made across the north side of the park in 1875. Opposite the end of Endymion Road, Williamson's Tile and Brickworks had developed into quite a large site with fourteen workmen's cottages and buildings. The Tottenham & Hampstead Junction Railway which opened in 1868, and from 1870 was run by the Midland Railway Company, also crossed Green Lanes; the station, originally Harringay Park, opened in 1880 in anticipation of serving the new district of Harringay. Beans Green stretched from the Tile Kilns to Hangar Lane, or what is today known as St Ann's Road. Beyond Hangar Lane, the Woodlands Park Estate, in West Green, developed in the 1880s, but only a few villas appeared on Green Lanes.

In the twenty years up until 1900 the whole area either side of Green Lanes was converted from open land to a densely built up suburban district. (Fig 2) Harringay as a district first appeared in Kelly's street directories around 1890. The name Harringay and its relation to the present day Borough of Haringey causes much confusion. It is very probable that the name Harringay derived from Heringes-hege, which in Old English means the enclosure of "Hering". The earliest written form of the name was recorded as Harenhg' in the twelfth-century and subsequent forms included at least 162 recorded variations, one of which was Hornsey. By the seventeenth century, Harringay and Haringey were both used interchangeably as names for both the village and the parish of Hornsey. By the late nineteenth-century Harringay had became the popular form for the name of the district around Harringay House, which stood on the west side of Green Lanes. Haringey, on the other hand, was used for official purposes and in 1965, the three Boroughs of Hornsey, Tottenham and Wood Green were amalgamated into one London Borough named Haringey.

The centre of Harringay is today focused on the stretch of Green Lanes between Finsbury Park and St Ann's Road. The whole area was developed as three separate estates. The Finsbury Park Estate, opposite the Tile Kilns, was a small estate of houses with shops fronting Green Lanes, including the Beaconsfield Public House. The Harringay Park Estate, the southern end of which came to be known as the Harringay Ladder. On the other side of Green Lanes the Provident Park Estate developed on the land of St John's Farm to become what is now known as Harringay Gardens. The shopping centre of Harringay on Green Lanes itself was developed in two ways; on the Tottenham side a single development resulted in Grand Parade, and on the Hornsey side as a series of uncoordinated, separate developments resulted in a variety of parades of shops.

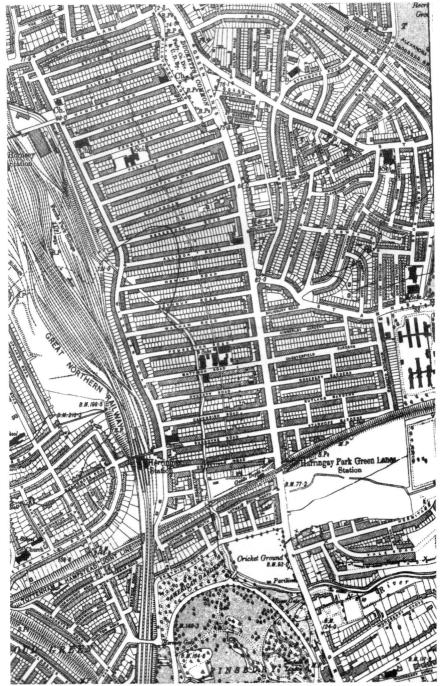

*Fig 2 Map of the area after 1900 (Taken from HHS map of Hornsey in 1920)*

Fig 3 *The frontage of the Beaconsfield with Benjamin Disraeli's portrait* (*John Hinshelwood*)

# 2

# The Finsbury Park Estate

The first development along Green Lanes began in July 1879 when Charles Hambridge, an architect of Guilford Street, Russell Square, submitted plans to the Tottenham Board of Health for a terrace of shops to be built between Endymion Road and Lothair Road. These first buildings on Green Lanes appeared in the 1880s as Sybil Terrace, with Sybil Mews behind them.

Following Hambridge's application, Alexander and Gibbon, a rather obscure firm of public house architects, acting on behalf of John Kemp, of the Railway Tavern, West Green Road, applied for permission to build the Beaconsfield in July 1880, although it was not built until about 1886. Presumably, John Kemp saw the possibility of expanding his trade to the future occupants of the estate which Hambridge was developing. The Beaconsfield public house on the corner of Lothair Road was the first public house to be built on Green Lanes, after the Queens Head on Duckett's Common, which is the oldest pub in the area.

The pub is named in honour of Benjamin Disraeli (1804-1881), the Earl of Beaconsfield, the Tory Prime Minister, whose portrait can be seen on the pub sign (Fig 3). The exterior of the pub has decent carvings of sunflowers in cartouche in addition to the primrose leaves, and a handsome projecting cabled stack on the Lothair Road elevation. The carved frieze of primrose leaves around the base of the first floor bay alludes to the Primrose League, a Conservative Party organisation formed in 1883, suggesting that the activists met here. Primroses were also a favourite flower of Disraeli, and he received them regularly from Queen Victoria.

The interior is slightly changed from the original; the centrally placed bar serving all areas of the pub was a modification in 1897, and the partitions between areas were removed at various times from 1904 onwards. However, the interior retains the fire surround and some stained glass.

Charles Hambridge laid out the Finsbury Park estate 1879 as the group of roads between Endymion Road and Lothair Road and all the roads were named after novels by Benjamin Disraeli so, like the Beaconsfield, the estate is a commemoration of the Prime Minister. Hambridge (1828-1883) was an architect who designed several houses in the 1860s for the landowner and developer, Henry Rydon, in Highbury, as well as the church in Highbury New Park. The Survey of London: also records that he designed a three storey full-blooded Victorian Gothic semi-detached house called St. David's for his friend Thomas Cree, a solicitor in the firm of Cree and Last. Helen Long, in her book "*Victorian Houses and their Details*", claims he was one of those architects who exemplified the high Victorian eclecticism in house styles in London in the 1860s. However, what has not been recorded before is that he also engaged in developments of his own, first on the Brownswood Park Estate in South Hornsey in the 1870s, and then on the Finsbury Park Estate in Harringay the 1880s.

Hambridge bought up the small plot of land that had become isolated by the two railway lines – the GNR running north from Kings Cross and the Tottenham & Hampstead Junction Railway running east to west across Green Lanes – and Endymion Road and Green Lanes. This was land originally earmarked by the Metropolitan Board of Works when considering the creation of Finsbury Park, but cut off from it by Endymion Road in 1875. Hambridge laid out the residential estate, divided in two by the New River to avoid the expense of paying the New River Company for a bridge. The new roads Lothair, Tancred,

Fig 4 The single style of terraced of housing on the Finsbury Park Estate

Conningsby and Ventia, named in honour of Disraeli, were laid out in a grid between Green Lanes and another new road – Alroy Road – beside the GNR. Houses on these new roads were then built between 1880 and 1882 by five builders whom Hambridge had worked with before; Thomas Grubb, William Hardy, William Piercy, John Thomas Pengelly Roach and William Garside. The houses all have the same architectural elevations and decoration and are easily recognised today as a single development built to Hambridge's design. (Fig 4) The development of houses in Endymion Road was also Hambridge's work, and although somewhat larger they have a style of decoration similar to the smaller houses on the so-called 'Disraeli' roads. When Endymion Road was to be named, in 1881, Mr George Baker, a clerk for a gold merchant, who lived on the road next door to William Piercy, asked for it to be called Jesmond Road but the Hornsey Local Board sided with Hambridge in calling it Endymion Road. The Finsbury Park Estate is a good example of an architect planned and developed residential housing estate aimed at providing good quality, yet uniform, housing for the middle classes.

*Fig 5 Harringay House by unknown artist. (Bruce Castle Museum)*

# 3

# The Harringay Park Estate

The next residential estate to begin, after Hambridge's estate, was what is now known as the 'Harringay Ladder'; the grid of streets north of Finsbury Park that appear on the map as rungs of a ladder between Green Lanes and Wightman Road. This estate, like Hambridge's, was built on either side of the New River which was straightened and tunnelled under the hill on which Harringay House stood (Fig 5), now the summit of Allison and Hewitt Roads, at the mid-point of the Ladder. Harringay House and all its grounds beside Green Lanes were acquired by the British Land Company in 1880 and a new road – Wightman Road – was made from Turnpike Lane to join up with Alroy Road. The streets of the 'Ladder' were then laid out to be later developed by a succession of private speculative developers and builders. The initial contracting works for the streets was carried out by William Hodson, originally a brick maker in Dalston, who initiated many building developments so that by 1884 he was wealthy enough to live in Downhills, a mansion standing in its own parkland in Tottenham.

The British Land Company grew out of the National Freehold Land Society established in 1849 by three members of the British parliament, John Bright, Richard Cobden, and Josiah Walmsley, to circumvent the restriction on voting. In mid-19th-century England, the right to vote was reserved for male landowners only. The trio established the National

Freehold Land Society, with the purpose of acquiring property and selling shares so that shareholders were then able to claim the property ownership right to vote. The society was later registered as the National Building Society and, like all building societies, was not legally allowed to own land, so, in 1856, Cobden and Bright established the British Land Company for this purpose. By 1878, British Land had paid off its debts to the National Building Society and become an independent and, eventually, publicly listed company. The 'Harringay Ladder' was one of the first large scale developments by this new company, and building plots were auctioned off on the new streets in a series of four or five auctions between 1882 and 1885.

The northern end of the 'Ladder', near Turnpike Lane, was initially developed as the Hornsey Station Estate, since the first plots of land sold were close to the Hornsey Station. The southern portion of the 'Ladder', beside Green Lanes was the called Harringay Park Estate, probably because the Harringay Park Station had also opened on Green Lanes in 1880. On the Harringay Park Estate the first houses appeared in Umfreville Road following an application to build houses to the Hornsey Local Board in March 1883 by architects David Burnett & Herbert Eldridge, 14 Nicholas Lane, Cannon Street. The houses, numbers 64 – 88, were built by H.J. Laurence, 22 Newman St., Oxford Street. Thereafter, over the next fourteen years, a total of eighteen different developers and builders completed the houses on Umfreville Road. The same pattern of development occurred on the other streets on the Harringay Park Estate, although none involved as many different developers and builders as were involved in Umfreville Road. The last developments began on Pemberton and Seymour Roads in 1891, these were completed by 1898 and involved eight and eleven separate developments respectively.

*Fig 6 Typical variety of speculative housing on the 'Ladder' Roads*

One of the distinctive features of the housing on the 'Harringay Ladder' is the variety of style and decoration of the houses in any one road (Fig 6). The development of the 'Harringay Ladder' involved 163 different builders, either individually or in firms. Most of the builders were small individual concerns with 123 of them building between one and ten houses each to give a collective total of 241 house, an average of about two each. At the other end of the scale there were just four building firms that each built more than 100 houses, amounting to 816 houses in all. In between the two extremes, the other 36 builders averaged some 40 houses each, with the lowest count of 12 houses for one builder and the highest count of 86 houses for another builder. Given the large number of separate speculative developers and builders involved such variety is hardly surprising. Similarly the naming of the roads, contrary to common anecdotes, follows no discernable logic. Another feature of the 'Ladder' is Haringey Passage that marks the line of the Hornsey Outfall Sewer, built in 1870. Houses could not be built over the sewer in case their foundations damaged it, thus a gap appeared between the houses as they were built and the footpath was created.

The two 'Ladder' estates were more than just lines of residential housing. On the Harringay Park Estate the first St Paul's Church opened in an iron church at the corner of Burgoyne Road and Green Lanes, in 1883, with the Rev. J. H. Greaves as vicar. A permanent church, designed by G.M. Silley, was subsequently built and opened in 1884 on Wightman Road. The parish of St Paul's was enlarged in 1903 by the addition of a portion of the parish of St Ann, Tottenham, on the east side of Green Lanes and a mission room was built there and dedicated in 1904.

Opposite the church, the Station Hotel opened in Wightman Road, in 1893, becoming the second pub after the Beaconsfield to appear in Harringay. Early in 1891 the Primitive Methodists opened an iron chapel in Mattison Road which was replaced by a permanent church and hall in 1901. Many of the Methodist congregation at the Mattison Road Church moved to join the congregation at Willoughby Road when the church became Roman Catholic in the 1960s.

A Higher Elementary School, which opened in 1904, between Mattison and Pemberton Roads, was the second school on the Ladder. It consisted of a building with 600 places for junior mixed pupils and another for 300 infants. It later became Hornsey County School having a special centre and swimming pool attached to it.

An editorial in the Hornsey Journal of 1929 looked back to the time when Harringay was the scene of the first big, mass produced, housing development "under which houses came not as single spies but in battalions". This was a very different type of development from the relatively small and restrained speculative development by Charles Hambridge.

*Fig 7 Near Green Lanes Station, J. May*
*(Bruce Castle Museum)*

# 4

# The Provident Park Estate

On the other side of Green Lanes (Fig 7) from the 'Harringay Ladder' the 'Harringay Gardens' estate developed from the 1890s when contractors, Harman Brothers of the City, laid out the grid of streets for the Provident Association of London Limited.

The company was established in 1877, in Lombard Street, London, by Baron (Joseph) Profumo, a member of an old Genoese family which was prominent in the commercial and financial world. The company offered a life assurance scheme whereby families of weekly wage earners, with little or no capital, could purchase a house which the Association had acquired. By paying a small weekly subscription, for five years, a man earned the right to purchase a bond enabling him to borrow the whole cost of a medium priced house from the company. He was then committed to monthly premiums for another twenty-five years before the loan was repaid. In many respects this scheme appeared similar to those offered by Friendly Societies or Building Societies. The Association spread its operations far and wide, but in London its greatest concentration of activity was in Tottenham where it built its own estate of houses. This all looked fine at first but if the man failed to maintain the premiums or wished to withdraw from the scheme for any reason he discovered how hard it was to redeem his investment. Many people began to feel they had been misled into paying money into the scheme from which they got no benefit. By the 1900s many of the subscribers were describing the scheme as the greatest Victorian swindle.

Eventually two test cases were brought against the Provident Association. In neither case did the Provident Association address the charges that the plaintiffs were induced to accept the bonds under the influence of gross mis-representation. The defence was simply that the plaintiffs had lost their chances of recovering money by accepting the terms of the bond. The judgement in these cases was that whilst the terms of the subscriptions might be understandable to those well versed in legal and financial matters, the mischievous practice of misrepresentation by the Provident Association of London prevented ordinary working men from recovering their money. The cases brought about a change in the company's behaviour. In 1905, a Board of Trade enquiry into Bond Investment Companies commented that the Provident Association of London was conducted on a sound system in which the company contracted "to pay after a term of years a lump sum which is equivalent to the amount of monthly subscription, with compound interest at a low rate, together in some cases with a bonus ascertained by actuarial value".

*Fig 9  St John's Farmhouse, St Ann's Road, H. Lawes (Bruce Castle Museum)*

The 'Harringay Gardens' estate in Tottenham was initially known as the Provident Park Estate, which was supposed to be a Garden Suburb, planned to the designs of the Provident Association's architect and surveyor, Thomas E. Haines. The Provident Association had acquired the land from the owner of St John's Farm, one Frederick Bridgman Windsor, a wealthy landed proprietor of Hampshire, sometime before 1890 (Windsor was apparently a descendant of Richard Thomas of London and Tottenham, who died in 1786). (Fig 9) This farm took its name from the Knights of St John of Jerusalem who held the land in the seventeenth-century, as shown on the Dorset survey of 1619. Between 1861 and 1871, St John's Lodge, was where the young Irish Victorian novelist Charlotte Riddell lived with her fifty-year old husband Joseph, an agent for an American Stove manufacturer. In the late nineteenth-century the value of the land as building plots had probably increased beyond its value as agricultural land. Windsor, who lived off the income from land he held in a wide variety of places would have had an eye for the best return on his investments, and was no doubt in little need of persuasion to sell to Profumo. After the estate had been laid out the first 6 houses, approved by the Tottenham Local Board, were built in 1893 on Stanhope Gardens which was fully developed by 1897. The majority of the houses on the streets were built between 1896 and 1898, with Chesterfield and Kimberley Gardens being completed by 1900 and the few houses in Doncaster Gardens in 1902, by which time there were about 1,800 houses. No houses were built in Stanhope Gardens between Doncaster Gardens and Warwick Gardens where in 1904 St Paul's

*Fig 10  A uniform long line of terraced housing in the Harringay Gardens*

Church established a mission hall. All the streets were named as gardens to promote the idea that the estate had the character of a garden suburb, but in spite of this the houses were built in long lines of unbroken terraces giving a somewhat regimented appearance to the estate.

With the exception of Stanhope Gardens, one side of Kimberley Gardens and a few in Chesterfield Gardens, all the houses have the same architectural style and decoration, which gives the estate a uniform feel rather like the Finsbury Park Estate (Fig 10). The grid pattern of the five principal streets between Warwick Gardens and Green Lanes is intersected by five staggered interconnecting streets, only a few of which have houses on them. This means there is no road from north to south, other than Warwick Gardens. The attractiveness of the estate as a suburban garden village for working-men's families was somewhat overshadowed by the neighbouring North Eastern Fever Hospital – now called St Ann's – beside Warwick Gardens, which was opened by the Metropolitan Asylums Board in 1892 to treat patients suffering from fever and diphtheria. If it failed as garden estate it succeeded, in spite of the company's reputation, in exploiting the need for new housing in a fast developing suburb, and returned a handsome profit for the company.

*Fig 11 The Harringay Park Granary building at 429 Green Lanes in 2010*

# 5

# The development of Green Lanes

The first shop, after Sybil Terrace and the Beaconsfield pub, to appear on the Hornsey side of Green Lanes was the Harringay Park Granary built by G.L. Wilson of Tottenham in 1884 at what is now number 429 Green Lanes on the corner of Cavendish Road. (Fig 11) This was the first of many small developments along this side of Green Lanes, which began in earnest in 1890 with the parades of shops between Lothair Road and the railway and between Umfreville and Burgoyne Roads. Both these parades, built in 1890, were designed by architect Thomas Mulbourne and built by H. Wickes. Cavendish Parade, the best preserved and most ornate of all the Parades, was built in 1892 to the designs of the architect Eugene C. Beaumont, for H. Linzell. Thereafter all the other parades, apart the one between Pemberton and Warham Roads, designed by the architects Bean, Burnell & Claridge in 1894, were piecemeal developments involving between two and five developers; hence the variety of styles of buildings between and amongst each parade. The last stages of development were in Seymour Parade, in1897, and Duckett Parade in1898.

On the opposite side of the road the development was very different. The first building to appear was the bank on the corner of Stanhope Gardens in 1894. (Fig 12) This was originally the London Provincial Bank, the initials of which can still be seen above the doorway. It was

*Fig 12 The original Bank building with houses behind on the corner of Green Lanes and Stanhope Gardens*

built by Mattocks Brothers for the bank, as were the few houses behind it in Stanhope Road. Other than the bank, the parade of shops which extends along the Tottenham side of Green Lanes is called Grand Parade; it was designed and built by the local builder John Cathles Hill, and was perhaps the finest late Victorian shopping centre in the whole of North London when it was completed in 1899.

At the age of 21 J.C. Hill moved from Scotland to 9 Albert Road, Tottenham. Four years later, in 1886, his success as a builder enabled him to move to a pseudo-gothic mansion called Southwood Hall in Highgate. As a builder and developer Hill found himself limited by a shortage of bricks, a problem he resolved by acquiring and developing a brickfield at Fletton, Bedfordshire, in 1889, where he built a huge kiln, called 'Napoleon' which was the biggest in the world. This was to eventually became the London Brick Company. In 1910 Hill founded a national association of brick manufacturers to try and tackle the trade's endemic competition which had been threatening its ruin. However, this had little success and by 1912 Hill was declared bankrupt with a deficit of over one million pounds. Hill died of a heart attack on 5 April 1915 and is buried at Highgate Cemetery.

The most impressive aspect of Grand Parade is the Salisbury Hotel, opened in 1899. The name Salisbury Hotel commemorates the Marquis of Salisbury, Disraeli's Foreign Secretary, and is a fitting counterpart to the Beaconsfield at the other end of Harringay. Hill also built the remarkable Queens Hotel at Crouch End which in many respects can be regarded as a twin to the Salisbury.

As well as the Salisbury and Grand Parade, Hill also built all the houses in Salisbury Road, one side of Kimberley Gardens as far as number 79, built as an attractive block of flats and the first half a dozen in Chesterfield Gardens. These developments were not part of the Provident Park Estate and the land was acquired separately from William Bradshaw who must have sold it at the same time that Hill acquired the common land of Beans Green along Green Lanes for the Grand Parade. The distribution of Hill's houses shows the demarcation of the Shoulder of Mutton Field which Bradshaw owned at the junction of Green lanes and St Ann's Road. Like Frederick Windsor, Bradshaw would have no doubt calculated that the monetary value of the small field was greater as building land than as an agricultural field. The style of Hill's houses in Salisbury Road, Kimberley Gardens and Chesterfield Gardens is very different from the style of houses in the 'Gardens'.

*Fig 13 Green lanes from Umfreville Road 1910 (Dick Whetstone)*

Grand Parade was built on the narrow strip of common land between Green Lanes and Provident Park as a single development of shops all with accommodation above them having a single architectural style. Each individual building in Grand Parade had a parade of shops on the street level with three flats above each shop. These flats were leased or let out as residential accommodation, in much the same way that the houses on the estate behind were. Access to the flats was by means of a separate doorway to the side of the shop. This was a similar arrangement to the various accommodations above the shops on the other side of Green Lanes, however, the unity of the design of Grand Parade contrasts strongly with the fragmented appearance of the parades of shops opposite; at the time it must have been one of the finest parades of shops in London. (Fig 13)

By the end of the century a few shops had also appeared beside the entrance to the Midland Rail Goods Depot beside the railway bridge; a coal merchants, a coffee house, a tailors and a tobacconist. Trams ran up and down Green Lanes, amongst the horse drawn traffic, bringing people to the new shopping centre. Harringay was firmly established as a new suburban district of London.

*Fig 14.1 Williamson's Potteries on Green lanes showing the tile kiln in the background which is roughly where McDonalds restaurant is today (Bruce Castle)*

*Fig 14.2 View of the site of Williamson's Potteries on Green Lanes today from the end of Lothair Road*

# 6

# How Harringay Changed

❦

Harringay has undergone changes in last the hundred years. The population has changed from a mix of artisans, clerks and shopkeepers of mainly English origin to a population, according to the Harringay and St Ann's ward profiles, made up of mainly professionals, managers and teachers. Those occupied in administration, trades and sales now only amount to about thirty percent and those in more manual occupations around fourteen percent. This diversity is also seen in the ethnic origin of the population. Around forty percent are white British, with another twenty percent of other white origin. Black British make up about eighteen percent and Asian about ten percent.

Not surprisingly the change in population has brought with it a change in the nature of the shops along Green Lanes. Comparing the categories of shops between 1908 and 2010 shows a great increase in the number of restaurants, cafes and take away food shops which is almost exactly matched by the decline in clothing shops. The number of individual food shops such as butchers, bakers and dairy products has declined to be replaced by small supermarkets. Hairdressers, and estate agents have multiplied and new betting shops, jewellers and shops selling electronics have all appeared. Although there are still plenty of shops selling household goods and DIY supplies the number has almost halved since 1908. There are no longer any bookshops and the number of news-agents has declined. However, apart from the changes to the nature of the shops and corresponding changes to shop fronts at street level, the overall appearance of the parades above street level is much the same as it was in 1900.

The most significant change to the street scene is seen at Harringay Arena Retail Park, named after the Harringay Stadium and Arena that stood here. ( Figs 14.1, 14.2) A small plaque on the wall briefly records the history of the old Arena and Stadium that stood on the site of the old Tile Kilns and the fourteen workmen's cottages that stood there. (Figs 15.1, 15.2) The name of Williamson Road also commemorates the name of the W. J. Williamson who ran the Tile Kiln and Brickworks. The Harringay stadium hosted dog racing from 1927 and may well have been unremarkable but for fact that the track housed, what is now, the only surviving automated totaliser in Britain. Curators at the Science Museum have preserved the machinery as one of the earliest examples of an on-line, real time data processing and computing system.

Railway Fields on the opposite side of the road, with its splendid, modern, wrought iron gates is now a nature reserve and teaching centre. It used to be the goods and coal siding for the railway until 1967.

Some traces of the early nineteenth century shops can still be seen. In the carriage-way entrance between numbers 73 and 74 Grand Parade is a notice by Frith & Co. who were the major architects, surveyors, auctioneers, house and estate agents in the area in 1908. They occupied number 70 Grand Parade. In 1910, these premises also included the National Telephone Co public call office, collectors for the Metropolitan Water Board (New River Co) and Tottenham Urban District Council.

Number 74 Grand Parade was where a furniture shop was opened by Mr Disney in 1913, before moving to the present shop. Originally, before Disney's took over the corner shop in 1938 it was occupied by Hughes Bros, as their Temple of Fashion, then by Taylors, a house furnishers. Disney's store now has the oldest shop front on Green Lanes and it is a

Fig 15.1 *This view of Williamson's cottages also shows the roof of Sybil Terrace, on the other side of Green Lanes, visible in the left background. This roof line makes it possible to identify the site of the cottags as the present day Williamson Road. (Bruce Castle)*

Fig 15.2 *The site of Williamson's cottages today taken from the car park of the Harringay Arena retail park.*

Fig 16.1 Hughes Temple of Fashion in 1910 (Dick Whetstone)

good example of an early nineteenth century department store. (Figs 16.1, 16.2) In 1953 the Disney family sold out to George Smith who ran the business until the Disneys bought the company back in 1985. The three Disney sons still run the shop.

On corner of St Ann's Road, opposite the Salisbury, stood the Electric Coliseum cinema that opened in 1912, and closed in 1961, and after periods as a Bingo club and a warehouse the derelict building was pulled down and replaced by the present block of flats. (Figs 17.1, 17.2) The parade of shops beyond, called the Salisbury Promenade, was built in 1920s. Woolworths was here in 1935, but moved to where the Iceland store now is in 1985, and now Tesco have a store there. When the Piccadilly line was to be extended from Finsbury Park in 1929 the Harringay Ratepayers Association campaigned for a station to be built here, but the railway company insisted that it would reduce the average speed on the line to an unacceptably low value.

Fig 16.2 Disney's store in 2010

The three residential estates have seen little in the way of change, apart from the replacement of some houses by blocks of flats as a result of clearance due to bomb damage in the Second World War. Many of the houses have undergone improvements the most visible signs of which are the installation of double glazing to windows in plastic frames, and the building of loft extensions. In spite of these changes the character of the street scene is still much the same as it was originally, although the numbers of cars kept on the streets has risen to saturation level requiring the area to have stringent parking controls. In an article in the Guardian of 2 March 2000 the area was said to be an "outbreak of life between Hornsey and Tottenham", and, although,

"The dog track has gone ... in its place there's real graffiti, proper fruit'n'veg shops and ...a paradise of sorts. ...Everyone wants to live in ... Harringay ... not least because of the great Turkish food on offer in the cafes and shops".

Fig 17.1 Green Lanes showing the Coliseum Cinema (Dick Whetstone)

Fig 17.2 Green Lanes showing the Coliseum flats 2010

Fig 18 Green Lanes during the
2009 Harringay Food Festival

Ten years on its still a good description of the district where a truly cosmopolitan population lives together as a vibrant community.

Every two years there is a fresh outbreak of life in the form of the biennial Harringay Green Lanes Food Festival. Around one-hundred stalls line the road and traffic is diverted away from Green Lanes, which fills with people enjoying themselves. The festival, organised by a committee of local residents, celebrates the cultural diversity of Harringay. Apart from food stalls there are activities for children and a programme of music and dancing from across the world performed by children from the local schools. Although the nature of the shops have changed the Green Lanes remains the hub of Harringay.

*Fig 19 The Salisbury Hotel with all the original features intact*

# 7

## Green Lanes, Harringay
## One hundred years ago

☙

From the Street Directory of Hornsey, Crouch End
Highgate and Finsbury Park 1908 - 1909

322 Savage William Albt., stationer
324 Ferrari G.. confectnr.
328 Irion Martin
330 Abels Joseph
332 & 334 Hinde Alan Hamilton
⎯⎯ *Woodberry grove*
336 Finsbury Park hotel, Walter Emanuel Manning
340 Barnard Jonathan
342 Castiglione James Lawrence
352 Compton Alfred John Spencer
Private Lunatic Asylum: Frank Raymond King, B.A.CANTAB., M.R.C.S., L.R.C.P., medical supt.(Northumberland house)
356 Ruth Mrs.
358 Weaver Joseph
360 Lapthorn John
362 Leek Mrs.
363 Court Mrs.
364 Canthery Isaac
366 Contier George
368 Potter William
370 Brooks-Clarke Mrs
372 Holt Mrs.
374 Irish Mrs. E. R.
376 Wright James
378 Napier William
Fire Alarm
⎯⎯ *Hermitage rd.*
380 Purkiss FrankGeorge, general storekeeper & trade valuer
382 Shakespeare Harry, greengrocer
384 Swainston Miss M., confectioner
386 Collins Fredk.. dairy
388 ManvilleHy.,hair drsr.
WEST SIDE.
⎯⎯ *Endymion rd.*
329 Dawkins Henry,grocer
Fire Call
331 Earland R.C.. butcher
333 Pinnock Frederick, provision merchant
335 Sluce Mrs.,wardrbe.dlr
337 Elliott Arthur, confr.
339 Pattisson Chs..oilman
341 Coleman Richard, dining rooms
343 Basset John Gerald, baker, & post office
345 Standring Misses E. & S., costumiers

## GREEN LANES,

Finsbury Park N. MAP N 1, N 1A.

*From Manor House Hotel to Midland Railway Station.*

[*For the first portion of Green Lanes see our "Stoke Newington and Upper and Lower Clapton Directory."*]

EAST SIDE.

316 *Manor House Hotel*, James Swinyard
Metropolitan Electric Tramways Limited (depôt)
318a & 369 Loader William J., bootmaker
318 Thomas Titus, refreshment rooms
320 Rose Eugene, tbcnst.

347 Manor Drug Stores
349 The Bungalow, con-
   fectionery
351 AblettGeo., bootmakr.
353 French Linton, cycle
   agent
355 Stuckey Wm. Philip,
   confectioner
357 Garland Mrs.,beer ret.
359 *Braconsfield Hotel*,
   George J. Garland
   *Lothair rd.*
361 Charles Wm. George,
   dining rooms
363 Taylor Thos., tobcnst.
365 Barwell Robert, tailor
367 Elsie Madam, child-
   ren's outfitter
369 & 318aLoader William
   J., bootmaker
371 Byatt Herbt., fruiterer
373 Hinchliffe G. & Co.,
   coal merchants
375 GothardCharles & Co.,
   Lim. coal merchants
377TapeE.T.&Co.coal mers
379 Turner & Lisney,
   cement & pipe mers.

### GREEN LANES;

HarringayParkN. MAPN 1A.
*From Harringay Park
station,Midland Railway,
to Green lanes, Hornsey.*

WEST SIDE.
   Glynn S. & Co., coal
   merchants
383 Bartlett GeorgeRalph,
   coffee house
383bWalker Bros., tailors
383aTaylorArth.W.tbcnst.
   Fire Escape Station
   *Umfreville rd.*
389 Hewett Frank, confr.
393 Donovan Miss Ethel,
   blouse & costume ma.
395 Becker Frederick
   William, baker
397 BrookHenryEdwards,
   dairyman
399 Kingsley S. J. grocer
401, 483 & 507 Turner & Co.
   bootmakers
405 Mann David & Co.,
   butchers
405 & 445 Adams Percy,
   fishmonger
   *Burgoyne rd.*
407 GreenHarry,wine mer.

409 Wilks Frank, ham &
   beef dealer
411 Johns Benj., bootma.
413 Cross Wm., tobccnst.
415 RoylanceC.&Co.lndry.
417 Saluon Joseph & Son.
   oilmen
419 Stevens & Steeds,
   cheesemongers
421 Campbell A. J. tailor
423 Cross James Randall,
   furniture manufactr.
425 Seear J. J. & Sons,
   confectioners
427 Mott Joseph, bootma.
427 Lush & CookLimited,
   dyers
   *Cavendish rd.*
429 **MARTIN & SON,** corn
   merchants (Harrin-
   gay park granary)
431 Covere Miss Jane
   Elizh., coffee rooms
433 Dow Brothers, M.P.S.,
   chemists
433 Mahony John, teeth
   specialist
435 Greenway&Co.,prntrs.
435aWillment Robert
   William, draper
437 Hillier George Edwin,
   builder
439 Nottingham Hosiery
   Co.
143 Roper James, oilman
145 & 405 Adams Percy,
   fishmonger
447 Stuhlmann H., baker
   *Duckett rd.*
449 & 451 Baker S. Gent
   & Sons, drapers
453 Russell Alfred E.,bldr.
455 SchwarChas.watchma
457 Neale & Co., grocers
459 Palmer Jn. Hy.,confr.
461 Cohen George Alex.,
   M.B., C.M.EDIN., phy-
   sician & surgeon
463 AlldayFredk.,butcher
465 Chitty Arthur, fruitr.
467 Baker Hy.,fancy drpr.
   *Mattison rd.*
   Fire Call
469 Crossley Charles A.,
   undertaker
471 Welsh R. J., oilman
473 **MAY'S LIBRARY,** stationers & artists'
   colormen ; post, tele-
   graph & telephone
   office
473 Mitchell GeorgeRobt.

475 Hoare George Charles,
   house decorator
477 Green Richard,butchr
479 de Save Stephen, fea-
   ther manufacturer
481 Mann & Colborne,
   ironmongers
483 Hawker Mrs , lndrss.
483, 401 & 507 Turner &
   Co., bootmakers
485 George Mrs. Emily.
   servants' registry
485 & 487 Gruneisen Geo.
   & Sons, drapers
   *Pemberton rd.*
489 Tyler F. E., wine &
   spirit merchant
489 Batt Wm. Hy., buildr.
491 ChignellFrank.tbcnst.
491 National Telephone
   Co. Lim. (public call
   office)
493 Packwood Jn.,bootma
495 Jarman & Hillyard,
   provision merchants
497 Robinson R., confr.
499 Smith G.Davis,draper
501EasonJ.&Co.corn mers.
503 Cordelle Madame,baby
   linen warehouse
505 Tearle Fredk., butcher
507 Stedman&Co.,grngros
507, 401 & 483 Turner &
   Co., bootmakers
   *Warham rd.*
509 Gordon AlbertEdwd.,
   tailor
511 Norfolk Henry, iron-
   monger
517 WaltonCharlesHenry,
   dining rooms
521 Bishop Arthur & Co.,
   music warehouse
523 Smith EdgarF.,clothr
525 Bradshaw Benjamin
   Thomas, butcher
   *Seymour rd.*
EAST SIDE.
   *Harringay Park Sta-
   tion,Midland Railway*
   *Grand Parade.*
   PILLAR LETTER BOX
 80 Smith Mrs. Charlotte-
   tobacconist
 80 Webb Mrs.
 80 Graham John
 80 Strawbridge R., confr.
 79 Leheup Edward, wine
   merchant

GREEN LANES—continued.
78 TyneMainCoalCo.Lim.
78 Golding Reginald,pork butcher
78 Speechley William H.
78 Gardner Mrs.
77 & 67 Taplin George & Co., toy dealers
77 Major Mrs.
77 Reardon Mrs.
76 Tyler & Brasher, grcrs.
75 De Horne John
73 Menzies Mrs.
73 Lee Henry William
73 Lavers Mrs.
73 SINGER SEWING MACHINE CO. LTD. ; M. Clark, manager
73 Oxley Harry, theenst.
72 Schweitser Adalbert, motor engineer
72 Bayley Mrs.
72 Cocks Fredk. William
71 Stone William Bevan
71 Gibbs George
71 Edwards Misses B. L. & K. E., confectionrs.
70 FRITH & CO., archi- tects, surveyors, auc- tioneers, house & estate agents
70 National Telephone Co. Limited (public call office)
70 Brooker F. C.,collecto. to Metropolitan Water Board(New River dis- trict)(attends friday 2 to 3 p.m.)
70 Messum W.J.,collector to Tottenham Urban District Council
70 Page J. F. L.
70 Shury Harry
69 Damant Ernest, um- brella maker
69 Davies John
68 Rolfe George
68 Jannings Hugh
68 Belayeff Mrs.
68 Home & ColonialStores Limited
67 & 77 Taplin George & Co., artistic stationers
67 Edwards Ernest John
67 McGahey Charles
67 Forrester Alexander
LONDON & PROVIN- CIAL BANK LIMITED ; William Williams, mgr.(Bank buildings)

=Stanhope gdns.
66 Brown Robt., ironmgr.
66 Crose David
66 Gough Ernest Harold
65 Foyle William & Gil- bert, booksellers
64 Yates & Sons Limited, dyers
64 Knight Joseph
64 Tuer Mrs.
64 Morgan Harry James
63 Nelson James & Sons, Limited, butchers
62 Lee E.. greengrocer
61 Duval Wm. A.,bootma.
61 McGivern William
61 Charles Wm., musical instrument dealer
60 Angel M., picture dealr
60 Smith Mrs.
60 Bird Mrs.
59 Baker Alfred F, hosier
59 Trott Alfred
59 Taylor William
58 RenéMrs.Nellie,millnr.
58 Newson George
57 United Kingdom Tea Co. Limited
57 Stevens Miss
57 Duncan Mrs.
55 Emerton & Sons Lim- ited, dairy
56 Lusty Henry John
56 Chapman Mrs.
56 Canfal Richard

=Rutland gdns.
53 Thursby Thos., butchr.
53 Usher John Thomas
53 Hughes Thomas
52 Goodman Joseph, hair- dresser
52 Gray A., tobacconist
51 Domestic Bazaar
51 Elliott Misses
51 Coles Arthur
50 Grosse Mrs. corset ma
49 Bhuwalla A., fancy dlr.
49 Hanks Sidney
48 Berry N.,pianoforte ma
48 Riddle Arthur Albert
48 Baynton Charles
47 Martin E.J.,mantle ma.
47 Hodd Richard
47 Nobbs Mrs.
46 McGregorMrs.B.,confr.
46 Thomson William M.
46 Thomas Harry
45 Lennox Henry
45 Smith Douglas
45 Lane Edgar Peter

44 Smith Donald, draper
44 Wilkie Charles
44 Sowerbutts Wm. Hy.

=Rosebery gdns.
43, 42 & 41 THOMAS & COMPANY, GENTLE- MEN'S OUTFITTERS
43 Loveridge John
43 Hodgson Percival
43 Hines Robert
42aRawlins Mrs.
42bStanley John Wilfred
42cHartley Alfred
41cStainton William
41bHobbs Harry Roper
40 Hawes Frederick J., jeweller
40 Annetts Thomas A.
40 Lewis John Robert
40 Norris Charles
39 WaltersCharles,mantle warehouse
39 Woodward Robert
39 Fellows CecilLeadwell
39 Simon Mrs.
38 Cole Turner, milliner
38 Jackson Miss Ada, dressmaker
38 Batchelor Arthur
38 Pickering Robt.Russell
37 Lilley & Skinner, Ltd., bootmakers
37 Mountfield Reginald
37 Soden George William
37 Snell Charles
35 Pollard John Franklin
35 Bucksch Frederick
34, 35 & 36 Hughes Brothers, drapers

=Chesterfield gdns.
33 The London City & Midland Bank Lim. ; A. W. Ward, manager
33 Dale John
33 Marillat Mrs.
33 Sampson Henry
32 Allen Hy. Walt., florist
32 Grahl Otto
32 Reilly Mrs.
31 Perry Sydney, teeth specialist
31 Blight Arthur
30 Oceana Laundry Ltd.
30 Ray Mrs.
30 Paggi Mrs.
30 Morgan Miss
29 Stone Henry Walter
29 James John
29 Edmonds William

28 Lipton Limited, provision merchants
28 Oxley Mrs.
28 Bo.. 'n Harry
27 Allardyce Thomas J., baker
27 Tollard Charles
27 Claydon Ebenezer
26 Barrett&Sons,butchers
26 Barrett Misses
26 Rawlins Alexander, designer of Christmas cards
26 Wharmby Thomas
25 Boots Cash Chemists Limited
23 Stone Ernest Percy
23 McLaren Mrs.
23 Dodson Arthur John
=*Kimberley gdns.*
22 Imperial Cash Stores, grocers
21 Fleming Reid & Co. Limited, hosiers
21 Evans Miss
20 Rabbits & Sons Ltd., bootmakers
19 Youngs George, pork butcher
17 Wheeler Bros.,butchers
16 DavisJudahR.,fishmgr.
15 Boston Geo. Jas., gro.
14 Matthews AlbertEdwd.
13 & 14 Jones North & Co., drapers
=*Salisbury rd.*
12 Sanders Bros.corn mers
12 Constable Wm. Edwin
12 Cox John William
11 Meyer Joseph
12 Scott Mrs.
11 Martin Alfred, tobcnst.
11 Pritchard Mrs.
11 Cuthbert John
10 Vaughan Mrs. Annie. milliner
9 Pearks Limited,grocers
9 Lowe Alfred John
9 Markwell Mrs.
9 Sturdy Arthur
8 Deacock Horace E.. provision merchant
8 Donaldson William Jo.
8 Ullyett Frank
8 Fillett Thomas
7 Lee Mrs. Selina, fruitr.
7 Payne William
7 Hazel Mrs.
6 Eastmans Lion.,btchrs.
6 Holland George
6 Staite Albert Thomas
6 Waller Ernest John

5 Tong Wm. H., grocer
5 Allen Charles Edward
5 Mercer William Henry, insurance agent
4 Pirie Joseph, chemist
4 Hare Egbert Frederick
4 Wilson David
3 Joseph Louis, furn. dlr.
3 Andrews William
3 Fox Alfred
2 Henry Bros., hatters
2 Warman Percy Edwin
2 Cantwell William
1 Hill John C. & Co., house agents
1 Earl George Salisbury Hotel (exors. of the late Robert J. Brinkley)
Pope Albert Edward, jobmaster (Salisbury stables)
=*St. Ann's rd.*

**GREEN LANES,**
Hornsey N    Map N 2A,
M 2A, M 3A, M 4A.
*From Green lanes, Harringay Park, to High rd. Wood Green.*

**WEST SIDE.**
533 Friern Manor Dairy Farm Limited
535 GowansMrs.Elizabeth M., stationer
537 Parke Henry Charles, pianoforte maker
539 MaynardsLim.,confrs.
541 Purnay Walter,oilman
543 Jones Geo. L., bootmn.
545 Smith George H., furniture dealer
547 Collins Fredk., dairy
549 Adams Jsph., chemist
551 Jupp J. & Son, wine & spirit merchants
553 McSievewright Wm., baker
=*Hewitt rd.*
555 Seeker Sidney, pawnbroker
557 Manchester George, bootmaker
559 WebbWilliamBarnett, stationer
561 Knight W. J. & Co., tailors
563 Harris W. J. & Co. Limited, sewing machine manufctrs.
565 Ingham Robert,grocr.

567 Fox Samuel, confctnr.
569MoehlenbrockGottlieb, foreign provsn. mer.
571 Brodie George, steam grinding mills
573 The Ivy Shirt & Collar Dressing Works
575 Schiff Mrs. C.,tobcnst.
=*Allison rd.*
CONGREGATIONAL CHURCH
579 Salmon & Son, oilmen
581 Smith Henry & Co., shopfitters
577 StevensMissesM.&R., ladies' outfitters
579 Hick William,tobcnst
581 Home & Colonial Stores Limited
583 Harrison John E.. incandescent light fitter
585 Mapperley Colliery Co. Limited
585 Lewin WalterWilliam
587 Bourlet Alfred John, jeweller
589 Turner & Co. bootmas
591 Johnson Jack, confr.
593 Roh Wm., hair dresser
=*Beresford rd.*
595 Bambridge's, bakers
597 Matthews Samuel, butcher
599 BennettRobt,dairyman
601 Hudson Sidney Chas., chemist
603 Cases J.E.,hardware dlr
605 Gullen Walter Edwd., house furnishe
607 Martin WilliamJas... Hulme, grocer, & post office
PILLAR LETTER BOX
607aAlsford J. & Co., timber merchants
609 Appleby Fruk., printr.
609 **FRITH & CO.,** architects, surveyors, auctioneers & house & estate agents
609 Messum W. J., collector to Tottenham Urban District Council
611 Harringay Ratepayers' Association (The); I.Clegg, hon. sec.
611 Denchfield William, dancing academy (Beresford Lall)

*Street Directory of Green Lanes in 1908 - 1909*

**GREEN LANES—continued.**
611 Mallett, Robert Thos.
611a Harringay Liberal Social Institute ; J. Paterson, hon. sec.
613 Carter Henry
615 McMillan John
619 Hefferman James, L.R.C.P.I.,L.M.,L.R.C.S. EDIN., physician & surgeon

*...Edmingham rd.*

621 Grant Chas., builder
623 Smith yes Thomas
623 Smith yes Miss, costmr
625 Evans David
627 Capon Isaac Henry
627 Southcard William Rapsey, solicitor
629 Debney Mrs. H.
631 Taylor John C.
633 Mayo Frederick
635 True Charles George
639 Flower Arthur, pianoforte dealer

*...Fairfax rd.*

Fire Call
643 Flack & Sons, oilmen
645 Mills William, grocer
647 Read Walter, butcher
649 Read Walter, greengro.
651 Liverpool Victoria Legal Friendly Society
653 Kelsey Arth., tbcnst.
655 Shorney Miss Agnes, stationer
657 Hards Jn.,auction rms.
661 Hawker Mrs. Maria, laundry

*...Falkland rd.*

**Queen's Parade.**
1 Turner & Co., bootmas.
1 Cole E. Haward & Sons, tailors
2 Speakman Geo. Edwd., corn dealer
4 Hewett Frank, confr.
5 Graves Louis Hy.,tbcnst.
5 National Telephone Co. Ltd.(public call office)
6 Holland Henry Isaac, cycle dealer

**Green Lanes.**
677 Queen's Head, Robert Stanley Chatley
*...Frobisher rd.*
Fire Alarm
*...Turnpike la.*

679 The Wellington, Mrs. Annie Marshall

EAST SIDE.

*...Harringay rd.*

PILLAR LETTER BOX
Atkinson Ambrose, M.R.C.S.,L.R.C.P., physician & surgeon (Park view)

**Park View Terrace.**
1 Canton Henry, R.D.S., dentist
2 Osborn Charles
3 Fullstone Norman Thomas, builder
3 Edwards David
4 Temple John, artificial teeth specialist

**Colina Villas.**
4 Frohnsdorff Max
3 Dadd Mrs.
1 MacKellow Mrs. L., dressmaker
*...Colina rd.*

**Green Lanes.**
590 Davis Arthur William, photographer
592 Marjoribanks Robert Bruce, M.B., C.M. EDIN., physician
594 C. R. Sanitary Laundry Co. Limited

**Harringay Villas.**
6 Coombes,JohnS.,school

**Green Lanes.**
Godfrey Jsph. Linzell (Cranleigh house)

**Ipswich Terrace.**
1 Lawes Henry
2 Benwell Mrs.
4 Glynn Albert
6 Campion Mrs.

**Green Lanes.**
*...Park rd.*
Frogley Isaac Charles (Claremont)
Widdowson Frank Edmund (Sandhurst)
Niven Mrs. (Roseville)
Carey Miss (Clareville)
Cole Turner (Oakville)
Bailey Henry Benjamin (Colville)
Atkins Mrs. (Rosemary villa)
681 script Tutorial College J. Charles Bull, &c.

636 Howard William Hy., M.R.C.S., L.R.C.P., physician & surgeon

*...Harringay gardens*
Pearl Life Assurance Co. Ltd. (H. J. Sayer, district supt.) (Copeland house)
McDonnell Henry, assistant insurance supt. (Copeland ho.)

640 My even Frederick
Taylor William (Glen view)
Taylor M. & F. photographers (Glen view studio)

**Harringay Villas.**
4 Wadey Mrs. C.
2 Parkin Frank
1 Pinchard Miss Eveline, school
1 Jenkins Harry

**Green Lanes.**
Goodman George (Elm house)

**Wordsworth Mansions.**
1 Brittain Rev. Herbert, B.A. [curate of Christ Church, West Green]
1 Baker Leonard Edwd.
3 Barnes Charles Morby
3 Stafford Mrs.
3 Chappell Mrs.
5 Parsons Edward Kent
5 Herrick E. J.
5 Reiner Arthur
*...St. Margaret's aven.*

**Wordsworth Parade.**
6 Stanley Parkes & Brown, auctioneers
6 Dennett Ernest
6 Stutter Alfred Edward
7 Gibbs Alfred
7 Billett Mrs.
8 Bunn Mrs., fancy drpr.
8 Toser Samuel
9 Thiel Jsph. hair dresser
9 Yearley William
10 Thompson A.F., lndry.
10 Fisher Edward
10 Wright Richard
11 Thomas Herbert
11 Engels Charles, picture frame maker
12 Bowles Isaac
12 Bezant Richard
13 Hamilton Mrs., wardrobe dealer
15 Hill Herbert